GLOBAL EFFECTS

THE IMPACT OF SCIENCE, TECHNOLOGY, AND ECONOMICS IN SUB-SAHARAN AFRICA

TAMRA B. ORR

Published in 2021 by The Rosen Publishing Group, Inc.
29 East 21st Street, New York, NY 10010

First Edition

Editor: Siyavush Saidian
Book Design: Tanya Dellaccio

Photo Credits: Cover Farm Images/Universal Images Group/Getty Images; p. 5 https://upload.wikimedia.org/wikipedia/commons/7/79/Countries_by_GDP_%28Nominal%29_in_2014.svg; p. 7 (top) https://upload.wikimedia.org/wikipedia/commons/8/8b/Figure_1_Map_of_Sub-Saharan_African_Countries_Eligible_for_African_Growth_and_Opportunity_Act_%28AGOA%29_Benefits%2C_January_2015_%2816669298266%29.jpg; p. 7 (bottom) Kristof Bellens; p. 9 tschuma417/iStock Images; p. 11 Ben Langdon/robertharding/Getty Images; p. 13 (top) Roger Brown Photography/Shutterstock.com; p. 13 (bottom) SIMON MAINA/AFP/Getty Images; p. 15 2630ben/Shutterstock.com; p. 17 (left) VW Pics/Universal Images Group/Getty Images; p. 17 (right) Neja Hrovat/Shutterstock.com; p. 19 (both) Roel Slootweg/Shutterstock.com; p/ 21 Thomas Imo/Photothek/Getty Images; p. 23 (both) TONY KARUMBA/AFP/Getty Images; p. 25 Neil Thomas/Corbis News/Getty Images; p. 27 SEYLLOU/AFP/Getty Images; p. 29 Marco Di Lauro/Getty Images News/Getty Images.

Cataloging-in-Publication Data

Names: Orr, Tamra.
Title: The impact of science, technology, and economics in Sub-Saharan Africa / Tamra Orr.
Description: New York : PowerKids Press, 2021. | Series: Global effects | Includes glossary and index.
Identifiers: ISBN 9781725322448 (pbk.) | ISBN 9781725322462 (library bound) | ISBN 9781725322455 (6 pack) | ISBN 9781725322479 (ebook)
Subjects: LCSH: Africa, Sub-Saharan–Juvenile literature. | Technology–Africa, Sub-Saharan. | Science–Africa, Sub-Saharan.
Classification: LCC DT351.O77 2021 | DDC 967–dc23

Manufactured in the United States of America

CPSIA Compliance Information: Batch #CSPK20: For Further Information contact Rosen Publishing, New York, New York at 1-800-237-9932

CONTENTS

CHALLENGES AND POTENTIAL

Sub-Saharan Africa is a region full of both challenges and potential for growth. Tucked below the ocean of sand that is the sprawling Sahara Desert, this region is made up of 46 different countries. Stretching out over 8 million square miles (21 million sq km), it is so large that the United States, Canada, and Europe could all fit inside its boundaries. More than 1 billion people live in sub-Saharan Africa. Experts have predicted that the population will double by 2050. These factors often cause hardship for a large portion of the region's population.

Living in the poorest region in the world, many sub-Saharan Africans struggle to find enough food and jobs to survive. Fortunately, that picture is starting to change. Foreign investors are improving the economy, while a stronger focus on science and technology has given the area more hope for the future.

FAST FACT

GROSS DOMESTIC PRODUCT (GDP) IS THE MEASURE OF A COUNTRY'S TOTAL ECONOMIC VALUE DURING A YEAR. MOST COUNTRIES IN SUB-SAHARAN AFRICA STRUGGLE TO KEEP UP WITH GLOBAL PRODUCTION.

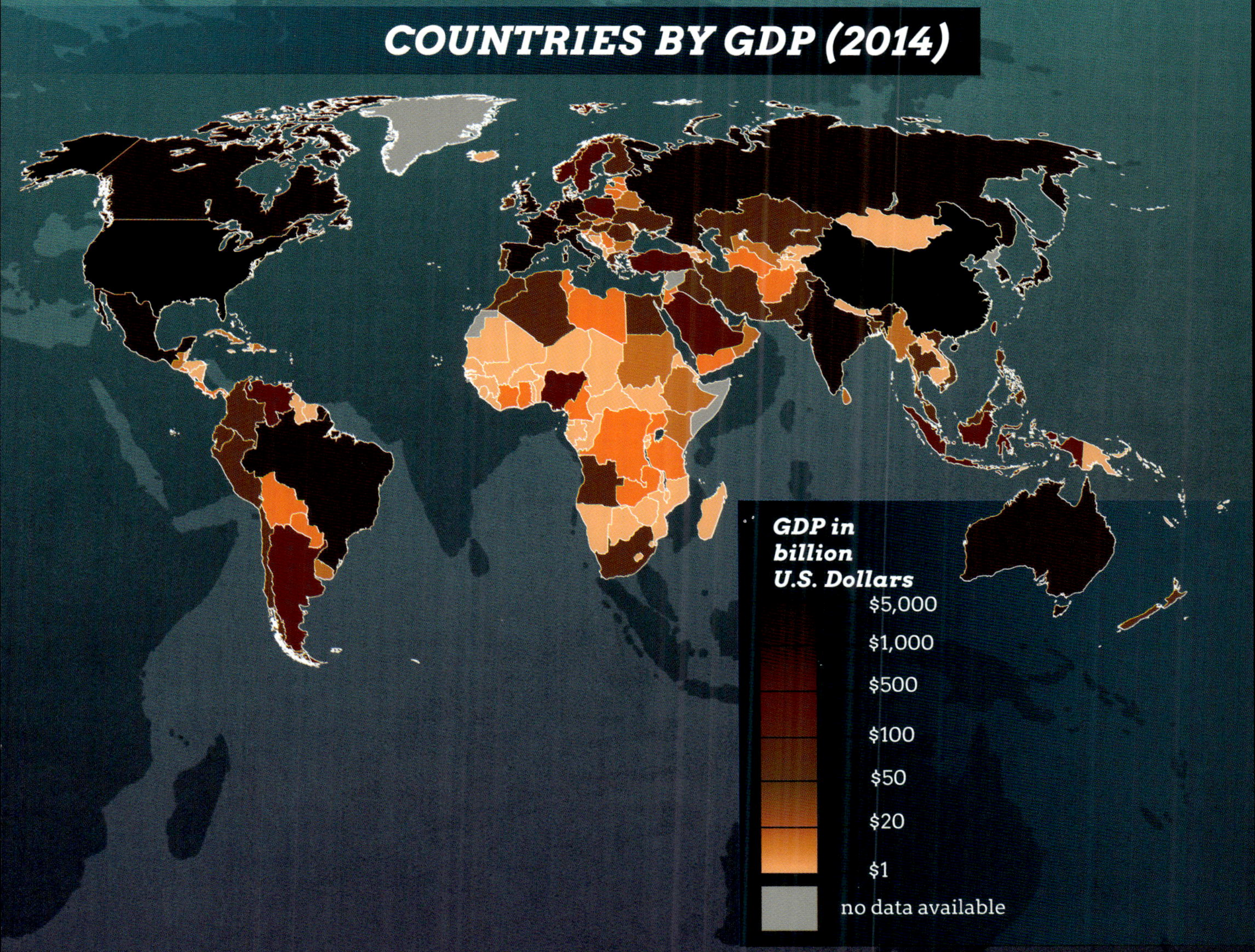

SUB-SAHARAN AFRICAN COUNTRIES HAVE SOME OF THE LOWEST GDP VALUES IN THE WORLD.

A SLOWER PACE

In 2015, economic experts predicted that sub-Saharan Africa's overall economy would climb at unusually fast rates. For a few years, it looked like they were right. The nation saw significant growth. However, in 2018, the growth rate dropped. It is gradually rising again, but at a much slower pace than originally **forecast**. This growth will also be uneven: 24 sub-Saharan countries—including Ethiopia—will see a 6 percent growth, while 21 others—including South Africa—will see less than 3 percent.

MAINLY A MIXTURE

The economic strength of sub-Saharan Africa changes from one country to the next. With 46 different countries sharing the region, one may thrive while others decline. More than half of sub-Saharan Africa's regional GDP comes from just three of its countries: Nigeria, South Africa, and Angola. These countries have a mixed economy, meaning that both the government and individuals can own and control the **factors of production**.

Unemployment in this part of the world is a common problem. Overall, only about 70 percent of the population has steady work. This number can vary between nations. In some countries, it is closer to 90 percent. In others, it is less than 60 percent. The majority of people work in agriculture, as sub-Saharan Africa **exports** a great deal of grain.

FACTORS OF PRODUCTION: CONDITIONS NEEDED TO CREATE GOODS AND SERVICES IN AN ECONOMY, GENERALLY LAND, LABOR, AND CAPITAL.

EXPORT: TO SELL GOODS TO ANOTHER COUNTRY.

FAST FACT

DESPITE IMPROVEMENTS IN THE ECONOMY, ALMOST 40 PERCENT OF SUB-SAHARAN AFRICANS LIVE ON LESS THAN $2 EVERY DAY.

SUB-SAHARAN AFRICA IS MADE UP OF DOZENS OF COUNTRIES, EACH WITH ITS OWN ECONOMY, HISTORY, LANGUAGES, AND BELIEFS.

CURRENCY: A SYSTEM OF MONEY IN USE IN A PARTICULAR COUNTRY.

COMPLICATED CURRENCY

Because sub-Saharan Africa has many nations, there are a lot of different **currencies**. In Ghana, for example, the basic unit of money is the cedi, while in Sudan, the currency is the pound. Zambia relies on the kwacha, and South Africa uses the rand. Nigeria uses the naira, and Eritrea the nafka. The currencies change quickly, with the images of new leaders replacing those of past leaders. The value of each nation's basic unit also changes frequently. Many people either **haggle** over prices or simply **barter** instead.

ECONOMIC VARIETY

Economically, the most powerful countries in sub-Saharan Africa are Nigeria, South Africa, Angola, Ethiopia, and Ghana. Even though less than half of the region's population lives in these countries, they account for more than 70 percent of the region's GDP. Angola is known for its oil production, while South Africa is known for its automotive industry. Ghana is the second-largest cocoa producer in the world, and Nigeria's film industry—Nollywood—is growing quickly. These nations are **newly developed**, meaning they're starting to become more industrial, with better economic and social health.

Many other countries in this region are **less developed**. They are limited by **infrastructure** problems. For example, some may not have access to the electrical power they need. Others don't have easy access to roads for transporting goods.

LESS DEVELOPED: NOT AS BUILT UP OR MODERN AS SOMETHING ELSE.

NEWLY DEVELOPED: DESCRIBING A COUNTRY WITH AN INCREASING AMOUNT OF INDUSTRY AND TECHNOLOGY.

FAST FACT

ONLY 43 PERCENT OF THE SUB-SAHARAN AFRICAN POPULATION HAS ACCESS TO ELECTRICITY. IN RURAL AREAS, THE NUMBER IS CLOSER TO 17 PERCENT. FOR COMPARISON, THE GLOBAL AVERAGE IS 87 PERCENT.

APARTHEID: A SYSTEM OF LEGAL RACIAL SEGREGATION THAT EXISTED IN SOUTH AFRICA, UNDER WHICH THE RIGHTS OF THE MAJORITY "NON-WHITE" INHABITANTS OF THE COUNTRY WERE RESTRICTED.

OUTSIDE FACTORS

There are many elements that affect local and regional economies. In sub-Saharan Africa, those elements typically include governments changing frequently and civil wars over land being fought repeatedly. It can be difficult to even survive in these situations—let alone grow an economy. Additionally, climate change—including longer summers and less rainfall—affects farming in the entire region. Many nations are also still recovering from European influence and racist policies, such as **apartheid** in South Africa.

WITH WARMER TEMPERATURES AND LESS RAIN, CLIMATE CHANGE HAS MADE IT MORE CHALLENGING TO GROW FOOD IN SUB-SAHARAN AFRICA.

NATURE'S TREASURES

Much of the international economic success of sub-Saharan Africa comes from the region's extremely large reserves of natural resources. Experts estimate that this region contains 30 percent of the world's minerals. Of the world's top 30 oil-producing countries, 5 are in sub-Saharan Africa. More than 20 of the countries in this area are considered **resource-rich**.

Some of sub-Saharan Africa's most valuable natural resources are iron ore, gold, copper, precious stones—such as diamonds—and other metals, such as titanium, uranium, and aluminum. Other valuable exports include tea, coffee, cocoa beans, and tobacco. Sub-Saharan Africa's biggest export partners are India, China, the United States, the Netherlands, and Spain. The region spends more on **imports** than it makes with exports. This puts more financial stress on an already challenged area.

IMPORT: GOODS PURCHASED FROM OTHER COUNTRIES.

RESOURCE-RICH: DESCRIBING A COUNTRY IN WHICH MORE THAN 20 PERCENT OF EXPORTS ARE MADE UP OF NON-RENEWABLE NATURAL RESOURCES.

FAST FACT

ANGOLA PRODUCES NEARLY 1.5 MILLION BARRELS OF OIL EVERY DAY. THIS NATURAL RESOURCE HAS BROUGHT WEALTH TO THE COUNTRY, AS OTHER NATIONS THAT NEED THE OIL PAY HIGH PRICES TO IMPORT IT.

COFFEE BEANS ARE ONE OF SUB-SAHARAN AFRICA'S BIGGEST CROPS AND ARE AN IMPORTANT EXPORT FOR THE REGION.

A CLIMATE CHANGE CRISIS

Because many sub-Saharan Africans rely on farming and agriculture, the impact of climate change on the region is serious. As temperatures rise and levels of rainfall shift, growing crops will become much more difficult. Most farmers do not use any **irrigation** systems, instead depending on rainfall. Some countries grow large amounts of a single crop, such as corn, in South Africa and Nigeria. If climate change harms this corn **monoculture**, the agricultural economy of these countries could be destroyed.

MONOCULTURE: THE GROWTH OF A SINGLE CROP IN AN AREA.

IRRIGATION: THE WATERING OF A DRY AREA BY MAN-MADE MEANS IN ORDER TO GROW PLANTS.

REGION OF YOUNG WORKERS

The population of sub-Saharan Africa is young. More than 40 percent of its population is under 15 and only about 5 percent of people are over 65. In addition, the population is expanding at incredible rates.

More than half of these young people are involved in agricultural work, but there is a growing **migration** from rural areas to urban centers. This has resulted in a severe shortage of jobs, as only one-third of new jobs in the early 2000s were available for young people. Many open jobs are either low-paying or vulnerable—meaning positions that are temporary, casual, and unreliable. The region's overall unemployment rate is 6 percent, ranging from a low of 0.3 percent in Niger to a high of 27.3 percent in South Africa.

MIGRATION: MOVEMENT FROM ONE REGION TO ANOTHER.

FAST FACT

EIGHT OF THE WORLD'S TEN YOUNGEST COUNTRIES ARE IN SUB-SAHARAN AFRICA. AS THESE PEOPLE GROW TO WORKING AGE, ECONOMIES MUST BE READY TO HANDLE THE INCREASE IN WORKERS.

ONE OF THE JOBS GIVEN TO YOUNG GIRLS THROUGHOUT SUB-SAHARAN AFRICA IS CARRYING WATER FROM THE NEAREST RIVER BACK TO THEIR VILLAGES.

EDUCATIONAL CHOICES

One of the problems with finding enough jobs in sub-Saharan Africa is the region's unbalanced education system. Young people are often encouraged to attend college, even though many can't find good jobs after graduation. At the same time, many students are ignoring the **vocational** education programs offered by some governments, such as Kenya's Technical and Vocational Education and Training system. Government leaders are urging young people to pursue vocational training so they can learn the skills they'll need to fill jobs in the region's developing industries.

LEADING THE WORLD

Tired of trying to grab the limited job opportunities in their region, many people elect instead to start their own companies. In countries like Nigeria and Zambia, almost 40 percent of adults are either opening a new business or have been operating one for only a short time. **Entrepreneurs** like this are respected and supported by the people of sub-Saharan Africa, largely because of the hope that they will grow their businesses and create jobs.

It's hard to succeed as an entrepreneur anywhere, but especially in this region. Governments rarely support new businesses, and it's hard to get funding. That doesn't stop people from trying, however. The fear of failing that scares many new business owners is much lower in sub-Saharan Africa, occurring only half as often as in the United States.

FAST FACT

THE TOP REASON WOMEN IN SUB-SAHARAN AFRICA START THEIR OWN BUSINESSES IS TO EARN THE EXTRA MONEY THEY NEED TO SEND THEIR CHILDREN TO SCHOOL.

HERE COME THE WOMEN

Sub-Saharan Africa has the highest rate of female entrepreneurship in the world. In Ghana, Nigeria, and Zambia, women are more likely than men to become entrepreneurs. This is especially impressive since women in many areas are also expected to stay at home and raise children. In general, women have less access to bank loans for starting their businesses and fewer opportunities to network—or talk with other business owners or potential customers—in order to market their goods or services.

IN MANY RURAL AREAS OF SUB-SAHARAN AFRICA, IT'S NOT UNCOMMON TO FIND SMALL SHOPS OWNED AND OPERATED BY FEMALE ENTREPRENEURS.

THE CHALLENGES OF AGRICULTURE

More than 60 percent of the people in sub-Saharan Africa work in the agricultural industry. In some countries, it is closer to 90 percent. The reasons for these huge numbers are clear: the population is growing fast and most people don't get enough food. The economies of sub-Saharan Africa—even in **more developed** nations like South Africa—must continue to support and expand agricultural production. However, maintaining a strong dependence on agriculture is complicated. Cities and farms both need access to clean water. Banks have to be willing to give loans to farmers who are struggling to adapt to the effects of natural disasters and climate change. Entrepreneurs with new planting and productivity ideas need to be encouraged and funded.

A VARIETY OF CROPS

While a variety of crops are grown throughout sub-Saharan Africa, the most common are maize (corn), rice, potatoes, sweet potatoes, cassava, and plantains. Many farmers also raise livestock, including poultry (chickens and turkeys), pigs, sheep, goats, and cows. Because of the huge size of the region, different crops are planted in different countries and at different rates. For example, Western Africa produces more than 60 percent of the crops for the entire region. Southern Africa produces just 22 percent.

ONE POPULAR SUB-SAHARAN AFRICAN DISH IS FUFU, A COMBINATION OF PLANTAIN AND CASSAVA.

FAST FACT

IN 2018, MORE THAN 239 MILLION PEOPLE IN SUB-SAHARAN AFRICA—NEARLY ONE OUT OF EVERY FOUR—WERE **UNDERNOURISHED**.

MORE DEVELOPED: HAVING MORE MODERN FEATURES THAN OTHER AREAS.

NECESSARY CHANGES

Scientific **innovation** often comes from desperate situations. This is true throughout sub-Saharan Africa, which faces many modern issues—especially climate change. Millions of people, whether they work in agriculture or not, will eventually face climate disasters, such as flooding and drought. To survive, they will have to make significant changes.

Fortunately, people throughout the world have stepped in to help find solutions. Together, sub-Saharan Africans and international scientists are exploring ways to lower risk for the farmers that make up a majority of the population. Researchers are sharing information on crops that are easier to grow in rising temperatures and with less precipitation. People are also working to build water storage tanks and **reservoirs** to reduce the impact of low rainfall.

RESERVOIR: A USUALLY MAN-MADE LAKE WHERE WATER IS STORED.

FAST FACT

IN SUB-SAHARAN AFRICA, 60 PERCENT OF CHILDREN BETWEEN THE AGES OF 15 AND 17 DO NOT GO TO SCHOOL. INSTEAD, MANY WORK IN SOME WAY—OFTEN ON A FAMILY FARM—TO HELP THEIR FAMILIES SURVIVE.

FARMDRIVE

As one of sub-Saharan Africa's most stable countries, Kenya is known for producing innovations. Technology and business stars Rita Kimani and Peris Bosire continued that tradition when they founded FarmDrive in 2015. This platform helps millions of small farmers keep better business records. FarmDrive then uses this information to connect users with banks that may be willing to give them small loans. This money can be used to expand, repair, or maintain an agricultural business that has no other way to get a loan.

RAINWATER HARVESTING DEVICES CAN BE SEEN ON THESE HOUSES. THIS TECHNIQUE IS ONE OF THE BEST WAYS TO ADAPT TO THE REGION'S CHANGING CLIMATE.

GOING ONLINE

Sub-Saharan Africa is slowly catching up with the rest of the world in the use of mobile phones and computers. Owning advanced technology is often a good sign of economic progress, as these devices are expensive. In the more developed country of South Africa, 90 percent of adults own a cell phone. In less developed Tanzania, this number is closer to 75 percent.

This region has the lowest access to the internet in the world. South Africa is the only country in which a majority of people are online. As these nations develop economically, however, these rates will increase. Across sub-Saharan Africa, 80 percent of people believe internet access has improved education, and 63 percent believe it has helped the economy.

FAST FACT

EXPERTS PREDICT THAT BY 2025, MORE THAN 50 PERCENT OF THE POPULATION IN SUB-SAHARAN AFRICA WILL HAVE PAID ACCESS TO THE INTERNET.

RWANDA: A SUCCESS STORY

Like many countries in sub-Saharan Africa, Rwanda has seen a huge transformation thanks to expanding its internet access. In 2008, only the city of Kigali had any fiber-optic cables, which are used for high-speed internet access and communication. Just two years later, the entire country had a network of these cables, which helped business and education improve. In addition to more modern technology, Rwanda's population of people with an advanced education is more than 20 times larger than it was at the turn of the 21st century.

ALL ACROSS SUB-SAHARAN AFRICA, INTERNET ACCESS AND ADVANCED TECHNOLOGY USE ARE ON THE RISE. THIS WILL LEAD TO A GENERATION OF BETTER-EDUCATED AND MORE CONNECTED PEOPLE.

THERE'S AN APP FOR THAT

As access to mobile phones and computers spreads throughout sub-Saharan Africa, digital entrepreneurs are creating applications (apps) that are tailored to fit the needs of Africans. An app called Plantheus, for example, allows farmers to use their mobile phone cameras to photograph and diagnose crop diseases. Another app, iCow, helps herders keep track of feeding schedules, warns them when to be on the lookout for disease, and connects them to people who may want to buy or sell their cows.

Physical teaching materials can be hard to find in sub-Saharan Africa, but an app called Kytabu allows teachers and students to download textbooks directly to their devices. The SafeMotos app rates thousands of motorcycle taxi drivers throughout the region. It also allows users to call a ride using their mobile device.

INSIDE GROWING TECH HUBS

Thanks to increasing internet access throughout sub-Saharan Africa, active tech hubs have sprung up in newly developed countries, including in South Africa, Nigeria, and Kenya. These are centers that welcome investors, entrepreneurs, designers, and programmers to use their equipment, get help and advice, and learn new skills. These popular locations make it possible for sub-Saharan Africans to develop, expand, and improve their ideas before going public with them. In turn, their ideas create new businesses and improve the entire region's economy.

COMPUTER TECHNOLOGY IS SPREADING ACROSS SUB-SAHARAN AFRICA'S RURAL AREAS THROUGH THE USE OF SIMPLE OUTPOSTS LIKE THIS.

FAST FACT

BETWEEN 2018 AND 2019, THE NUMBER OF TECH HUBS THROUGHOUT SUB-SAHARAN AFRICA GREW BY 40 PERCENT, FROM 442 TO 618.

GOING TO SCHOOL

Getting a good education in sub-Saharan Africa can be challenging. In many countries, there are not enough places for schools, and not enough teachers even when space is found. Many of the available teachers have little to no formal training.

In places like Niger and Ethiopia, only one in four people have ever attended school. Those that do go to school often do not stay until graduation. By the time students reach high school age, more than half have stopped attending. This is especially true for girls, who tend to go to school for shorter periods of time throughout the entire region. Low-quality education often has a ripple effect. Undereducated young people will enter the workforce without enough skills, which hurts the economy, making it harder for governments to fund education.

FAST FACT

THE **LITERACY** RATE THROUGHOUT SUB-SAHARAN AFRICA VARIES FROM ONE COUNTRY TO ANOTHER. IT AVERAGES 65 PERCENT OVERALL, RANGING FROM A HIGH OF 90 PERCENT IN THE SEYCHELLES TO A LOW OF 19 PERCENT IN MALI.

IN SUB-SAHARAN AFRICA, MORE THAN 20 PERCENT OF ELEMENTARY SCHOOL-AGED STUDENTS NEVER ATTEND SCHOOL. BY THE TIME THEY REACH TEENAGE YEARS, THAT NUMBER INCREASES TO 34 PERCENT.

AFRICAN ROBOTS

Fundi Bots, a company headquartered in Uganda, has found a way to help people get connected with high-quality education. It offers school outreach programs that teach children subjects that will be useful in the region's advancing economy. Its main focus is teaching science, technology, engineering, and math (STEM) skills. In addition to after-school classes, Fundi Bots works with government educators to make STEM subjects a part of the national **curriculum**. In an increasingly technology-based world, sub-Saharan African children will need to have STEM knowledge.

SOLAR SCIENCE

For decades, sub-Saharan Africa has had to face huge challenges. The region is finding some solutions through advances in science and research. For example, many parts of this large area deal with electricity shortages, especially in the smallest, most remote, least developed countries.

One expanding solution has been found in the installation and use of small solar panels in people's homes. These devices capture power from the sun's rays and transform it into usable energy. They are popular in this region because they are reliable and inexpensive. Solar panel systems capable of powering everything from small phone chargers to a variety of household appliances have been installed in many of the larger cities. Sales of solar panel systems are increasing throughout the region. Each year, this renewable energy resource is reaching more isolated locations.

RELYING ON RICE

Population growth is common in developing regions, and sub-Saharan Africa is no different. Keeping everyone fed is a major problem. Scientists believe one solution might be found in the search for sturdier types of rice to grow. Rice is quick and easy to prepare and it's a good source of energy. Researchers are experimenting with a type of rice that grows fast, resists drought and pests, and grows in poor soil. Large rice crops mean more food to sell—and to eat.

FAST FACT

IN 2014, THE SUB-SAHARAN COUNTRY OF TOGO ONLY PRODUCED ENOUGH ELECTRICITY TO RUN A COMPUTER FOR 80 HOURS—IN AN ENTIRE YEAR.

THE INSTALLATION OF SOLAR PANELS IN PLACES LIKE SENEGAL IS MAKING A HUGE DIFFERENCE IN THE REGION'S ENERGY PRODUCTION.

MOSQUITOES, MALARIA, AND MORE

Diseases are a major threat to public health throughout parts of sub-Saharan Africa. **Malaria** is one of the region's worst offenders. This life-threatening disease is transmitted through the bite of a specific type of mosquito. In 2017, there were more than 200 million cases of malaria, and the majority of them came from countries within this region. Scientists, both locally and globally, are trying to find ways to prevent and better treat the disease.

Though life in sub-Saharan Africa can be challenging, some things are getting better. With more access to modern technology, education and health care have improved. Increased natural resource exports have boosted some economies, though the region overall must find a way to reduce import costs if it wants to continue its growth.

FAST FACT

THE GLOBAL COVID-19 VIRUS PANDEMIC, OR WIDESPREAD ILLNESS, THAT BEGAN IN 2019 THREATENED TO STRAIN HEALTH SYSTEMS AND ECONOMIES ACROSS THE SUB-SAHARAN REGION AND THE WORLD.

MEDICAL INNOVATIONS ARE NOT EASY TO PRODUCE, BUT RESEARCHERS IN SUB-SAHARAN AFRICA ARE TAKING ON THE CHALLENGES OF HEALING AND PREVENTING DISEASE IN THE REGION.

LIVING IN SUB-SAHARAN AFRICA

Life expectancy is how long an average person in an area is predicted to live. It is often used to measure how economically developed a region is. After all, a strong economy leads to more money, better scientific research, and improved medical care—all of which help people live longer. Over the years, life expectancy in sub-Saharan Africa has improved, but the region is still mostly less developed or newly developed. The overall average is about 61 years, with Chad (52) and Mauritius (75) on the low and high ends.

GLOSSARY

barter: To exchange goods or services in return for other goods or services.

curriculum: The standard topics taught in a school.

entrepreneur: A person who runs his or her own business.

forecast: Guessed about or predicted.

gross domestic product (GDP): The total value of the goods and services produced by a country.

haggle: To argue over the price of something.

infrastructure: The equipment and structures needed for a country, state, or region to function properly.

innovation: A new or better way of doing things.

literacy: The ability to read and write.

malaria: A disease caused by the bite of an infected mosquito.

undernourished: Lacking enough food to maintain good health.

vocational: Related to a specific job or career.

FOR MORE INFORMATION

BOOKS

Milson, Andrew J. *National Geographic World Cultures and Geography: Eastern Hemisphere*. Chicago, IL: National Geographic Learning, 2017.

Rector, Rebecca Kraft. *The Sahara Desert.* Mankato, MN: Focus Readers, 2018.

Wanner, Zukiswa. *Africa*. New York, NY: Children's Press, 2019.

WEBSITES

Africa Facts
www.kids-world-travel-guide.com/africa-facts.html
This website contains fascinating facts about Africa and links to explore further.

Ducksters: Africa
www.ducksters.com/geography/africa.php
This site offers details about Africa's geography, a coloring map of the continent, and links to each one of its countries to learn more.

South Africa Facts!
www.natgeokids.com/za/discover/geography/countries/facts-about-south-africa
National Geographic's website offers facts, maps, photographs, and more about this country within sub-Saharan Africa.

Publisher's note to educators and parents: Our editors have carefully reviewed these websites to ensure that they are suitable for students. Many websites change frequently, however, and we cannot guarantee that a site's future contents will continue to meet our high standards of quality and educational value. Be advised that students should be closely supervised whenever they access the internet.

INDEX